Kindred

Anne-Marie Flores

Kindred © 2022 Anne-Marie Flores

All rights reserved.

No part of this publication may be reproduced, stored in a retrieval system, or transmitted, in any form or by any means, electronic, mechanical, photocopying, recording or otherwise, without the prior written permission of the presenters.

Anne-Marie Flores asserts the moral right to be identified as author of this work.

Presentation by *BookLeaf Publishing*

Web: www.bookleafpub.com

E-mail: info@bookleafpub.com

ISBN: 9789357448369

First edition 2022

DEDICATION

To all I've loved. And to those who taught me to love. And to my little girl, who I'll love unconditionally when she arrives.

Day 1

There's a girl inside my head
A room with soundproof walls,
Open palms, pounding red
Away they walk, deaf to her calls

Her mother, father, lovers, friends
Brow furrowed, tear-stained face
They all left her long ago
Alone inside this place

When she lays her head to sleep
It's restlessness she finds,
And when she wakes there's screeching birds
It's noisy in my mind.

Day 2

"I've got you"
Is the safe space between us
It's the warm quiet that silences the noise
The healing you pour into my tired bones

"I've got you"
Is the navy suit and party charm
Dependable, by my side
The zip in my dress after a long night

"I've got you"
Is what you whisper
Wrapped snug in our afterglow
My spirit set free, unbound in worship

Day 3

I saw you on the big screen again today
All arms, legs, and big healthy stretches
Today you're 23 weeks old

The first time I heard your heart beat
It wiped away every doubt I had
Made all the pain and discomfort worth it

In 4 months you'll meet the world
Don't worry, I'll hold you close as much as I can,
So you're not alone for too long

Between now and then
Soothing my body and holding my mind
Looking at the blue of your little face and feet
Daddy's feet
We can't wait to meet you

Day 4

I crave the quiet
Too many cars, busses, trucks
Too much chatter, hollow

I crave the quiet
Peaceful, silence,
Even in my mind

Day 5

"I love you", never tasted so good on my lips
After pressing the words into your skin

Yours is my palate cleanser
Wiping away everything that stood before you

Here we are
A chance, every day
To begin again

Day 6

I pour over your cherished words to learn the
pieces of you
The dog-ears, the led scrawl, circled and lined
phrases, significance I try to glean
I'd like to see what's underneath
I long to be close

I kiss your brow, cradled in your seat
Willing my body to be still, to listen to your
body
I am stumped, a wall I cannot climb
I yearn to unlock in you what I have been given
before, vulnerable, cracking open
But what I give you don't receive and what you
give I don't receive

I pour over your skin to illicit response
But my touch to you is likened to a pleasant day
No more, no less
And in this way I lay dormant
Your touch to me like a pleasant day
No more, no less

Day 7

"You're not a princess, you know"
"Because of you I didn't have a good life"
"I didn't get a chance to enjoy my 20's"
"No dance classes. Because I said so."
"We'll be back, soon."
"They've left you here again."
"They won't answer the phone."
"I'll kill myself."
"You're wasting your money on therapy."

Day 8

Harris Park,
Sitting at Lola's dresser,
A tri-fold mirror,
Glass bottles of perfume delicately laid out; and
Lipsticks in different shades of red

Day 9

Gravelled voice at 2am
Kisses pressed into my shoulder
"Love you"

An omelette for breakfast
Peppermint tea
A crossword puzzle to share

Crying, again
Please, please, please
"Thank you"

Day 12

In the absence I draw imagery
Of worst-case scenarios
Not of a shared bed or lingering glance
But of laughter and endless conversation
Long into the night
I try to hold a candle up
To what you see in that woman,
Of what I used to be
But the darkness engulfs
My small light
And hers roars bright, so bright

Day 14

There's a special trick
To putting one foot in front of the other
It can be found in a teenage aunt
Or a drug-addicted uncle
A grandfather that only knows optimism
A corporate suit looking down on you
It's not found in 'good' or 'bad'

That 'something' is undying well wishes for you
The kind of love that stands in your corner.
Or that something is undeserved scorn,
And your humiliation fuels your ambition

It's the school fees anonymously paid for
The lunches miraculously appearing in your bag
A new uniform, books and the right coloured
socks
Sanitary pads when your first sign of
womanhood arrives
The hard push, the exile, to find true north

It's the broken pride in your father
The shame in your mother
Protecting them both and restoring their name

It's the hope for your siblings
The joy in your journey
The chance to rest that's surely just around the
corner

Day 16

Across a table
Heavy hearts
"I'm so tired", I say

A karaoke bar
Spilt words
Giddy, flushed cheeks

A park bench
The first kiss
Like teenagers again

A sky-high view
Lounge for two
"I'm in love with you"

The first tremble
The first rumble
The first roar

The pool
A stripped shirt
My proud smile

The quiet

Your chest
My heart

The distance
Stolen weekends
Making up for lost time

Our broken minds
Us, left behind

Day 17

Behind closed doors
Debauchery, kindness, companionship
Chasing the feeling of alive
More expensive than a roller coaster ride
Cheaper than a wife

Behind closed doors
A broken mind, unsaid words
Chasing the feeling of being understood
More expensive than the truth
Cheaper than the lie

Day 18

The last one picked for the team
The rubbish at the bottom of the heap
Good enough to bed but not enough to keep

17 Weeks

I am unequally horrified and amazed,
I'd say the ratio is two-to-one:
One part depression, one part repulsion, one part
cautious love.

A life has implanted itself in the walls of my
womanhood
I am softening, expanding, vomiting,
So much vomiting.

Pregnancy is not the glow from within that was
promised and glamorised
It is hyperemis gravidarum - not a spell I learned
at Hogwart's
It is isolating, debilitating, painful
It is pissing my pants and standing in a puddle of
wet, after emptying my stomach of the nothing I
ate
It is guilt
It is suffering
It is stepping back in my career
It is asking "when will I feel better?"
And a pitying smile that says, "maybe
tomorrow"

Ink Soaked

On the first page of my story, my pen burst, and like your blood, ink soaked through my chapters right to the spine. Years passed and the ink blot shrank, smaller until one day, there was only a faint mark, right in the centre. Fervent, I rushed to the end of my book, and there the mark stood firm, a fragment of the blood-soaked pages from years ago, but real and stubborn. Kindred to the spine, cover to cover.

September 2019

I once thought that I wasn't enough; enough for someone to stay, enough for someone to pray for, enough for someone to love. Now I realise that I am too much. I am boundless positivity and warm energy in every fibre. My light is searing, and it is telling. For every love I've had, I have given my all, and demanded the same in return. My knowing who I am, raised fear in men, less-sure of themselves. There's some kind of sublimity that's washed over me since understanding this. Love should exalt us, and love for myself has done just that.

Worship

Tongue on soft flesh over a life force standing
firm
I'm in my place of worship
God moves through us when we accept him.
Tears, after the earth shakes.
I see a hand held, secure and so sure through the
act of bring forth life
A chest to cry on and warmth in the cold, as we
welcome death.
I prayed to my God and he sent me a muslim
man.

December

21

Abandon, surrender - your chemistry forcing my
hand
This love transcending all logic
Every fibre, sinew in my body,
Has been in search of you.

"It's all just words", you'll tell me
But I've written you into existence
Over years
When I was convinced I'd fallen
Out of God's favour.

Suffering

This god-like man was bound to the bow of the ship without chains, as if there voluntarily. His face was anguished and filled with rage. From collarbone to pubis he was carved open - a great chasm where all his organs should be. In their place, molten lava of the earth's core, hissing with each violent wave that pushed up against the ship as it charged onwards.

8/12/16

I love you all, so very, very much. I am so sorry for disappointing you and losing my shine. I was supposed to be the strong one but I'm the weakest of the litter. You have all loved me enough, guided me enough, cherished me enough. Thank you for being the most wonderful bunch of human beings I have been blessed to call my family. I will miss you all very much.

www.ingramcontent.com/pod-product-compliance
Lightning Source LLC
Chambersburg PA
CBHW070733160726
48003CB00006BA/2480